STRIPES
of All Types

RAYAS
de todas
las tallas

For my wonderful siblings,

Sally, Ann, and Lee,

and to the memory of our beloved brother, Grant

Para mis maravillosos hermanos,

Sally, Ann y Lee,

y a la memoria de nuestro amado hermano, Grant

Published by
PEACHTREE PUBLISHING COMPANY INC.
1700 Chattahoochee Avenue
Atlanta, Georgia 30318-2112
www.peachtree-online.com

Text and illustrations © 2013, 2014 by Susan Stockdale
Spanish translation © 2014 by Peachtree Publishers

First bilingual edition published in hardcover, trade paperback, and big book in 2014.

Art direction by Loraine M. Joyner
Typesetting by Melanie McMahon Ives
Spanish translation: Cristina de la Torre, in collaboration with Susan Stockdale
Spanish copy editor: Cecilia Molinari

The author and publisher thank Lulu Delacre for her editorial support
on the Spanish translation.

Illustrations created in acrylic on paper; cover title typeset in Ray Larabie's Libel Suit; text typeset in The Monotype Corporation's Gill Sans by Eric Gill

On the front cover: striped skunk; on the back cover: common zebra

Manufactured in September 2021 by Toppan Leefung Printing Limited in China
10 9 8 7 (bilingual paperback)
10 9 8 7 6 5 4 3 2 1 (bilingual hardcover)
10 9 8 7 6 5 4 3 2 1 (bilingual big book)
10 9 8 7 6 5 4 (bilingual board book)

English / Spanish PB: 978-1-56145-793-9
English / Spanish HC: 978-1-56145-798-4
English / Spanish BB: 978-1-56145-823-3
English / Spanish Big Book: 978-1-56145-794-6

Also available in an English-language edition:
HC ISBN: 978-1-56145-695-6

Library of Congress Cataloging-in-Publication Data

Stockdale, Susan, author.
Stripes of all types / Rayas de todas las tallas / by Susan Stockdale ; translated by Cristina de la Torre.
pages cm
English and Spanish.
Includes bibliographical references and index.
ISBN 978-1-56145-798-4 (hardback)
ISBN 978-1-56145-793-9 (paperback)
ISBN 978-1-56145-794-6 (big book)
1. Animals—Color—Juvenile literature. 2. Camouflage (Biology)—Juvenile literature. 3. Stripes—Juvenile literature. I. Stockdale, Susan. Stripes of all types. II. Stockdale, Susan. Stripes of all types. Spanish. III. Title. IV. Title: Rayas de todas la tallas.
QL767.S76618 2014
591.47'2—dc23
2013039822

I am grateful to many scientists at the Smithsonian Institution's National Museum of Natural History for their valuable research assistance. They include Dr. Allen Collins, Dr. Kevin de Queiroz, Dr. Carla Dove, Dr. Jerry Harasewych, Mr. Gary F. Hevel, Dr. Dave Johnson, and Dr. Victor G. Springer.

I am especially thankful to Dr. Kristofer Helgen, also of the National Museum of Natural History, for his help regarding the many mammals in this book.

Agradezco a muchos de los científicos del Museo Nacional de Historia Natural del Smithsonian Institution por su valiosa ayuda en la investigación de este libro. Entre ellos, el señor Gary F. Hevel y los doctores Allen Collins, Kevin de Queiroz, Carla Dove, Jerry Harasewych, Dave Johnson, y Victor G. Springer.

Y quedo especialmente agradecida al doctor Kristofer Helgen, también del Museo Nacional de Historia Natural, por su ayuda respecto a los numerosos mamíferos que aparecen en este libro.

Stripes of All Types
Rayas de todas las tallas

Written and illustrated by / Escrito e ilustrado por
Susan Stockdale
Translation by / Traducción de Cristina de la Torre

PEACHTREE
ATLANTA

Stripes found in water,

Hay rayas en el agua,

sliding through weeds.

y deslizándose entre hierbas.

Drinking from rivers,

Bebiendo de los ríos

and darting through reeds.
y atravesando los juncos.

Toting a shell,

Cargando un caracol,

twisting on sand.
serpenteando por la arena.

Sprawled in a lair,

Tendidas en la guarida,

and sprinting on land.
galopando en las planicies.

Prowling the prairie,

Rondando por las praderas

perched on a peak.
y encaramadas en altas cumbres.

Crawling on cactus,

Caminando sobre el cactus

and camped by a creek.
y echadas junto al arroyo.

Propped on a log,

Trepadas en un tronco

poised on a leaf.

y posadas sobre una hoja.

Scaling a ridge,
Subiendo por el cerro

and scouting a reef.
y explorando el arrecife.

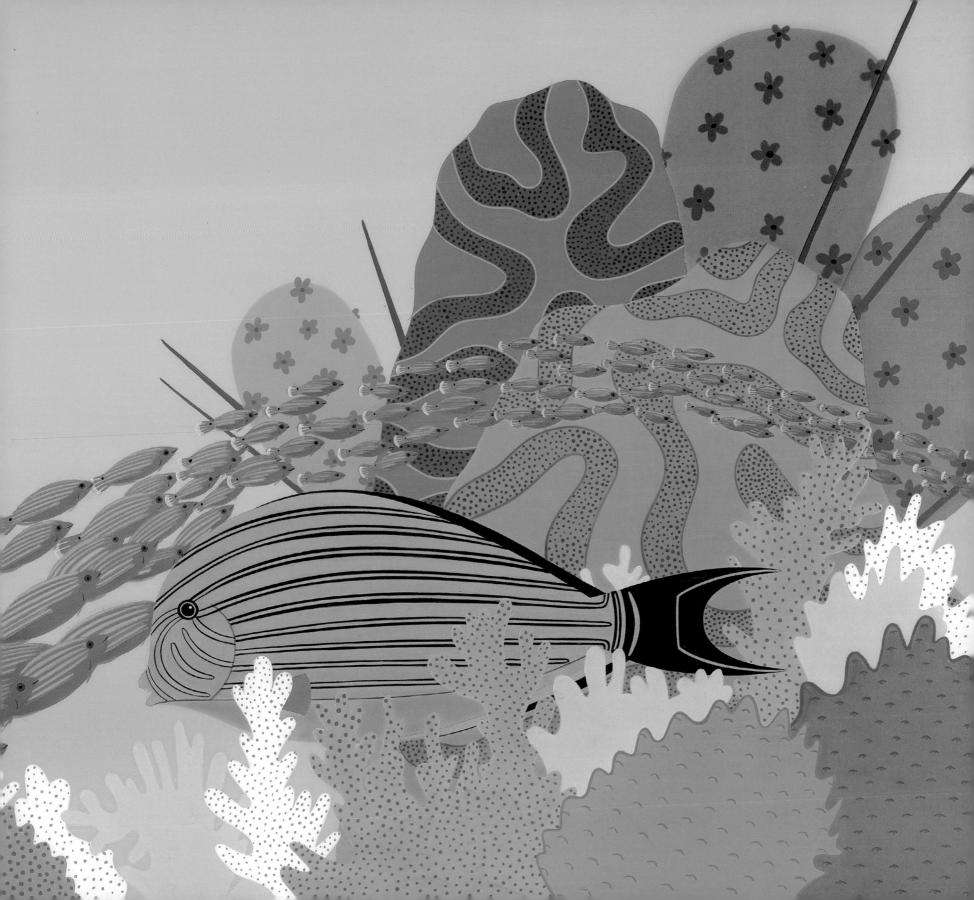

Stripes found in forests,

Hay rayas en los bosques,

stripes found on farms.

rayas en las granjas.

Stripes found with children,
curled in their arms.

Y hay rayas que los niños
acurrucan en sus brazos.

Can you find the animals that belong to these STRIPES?
¿Puedes decir a qué animales pertenecen estas RAYAS?

ring-tailed lemur / lemur de cola anillada

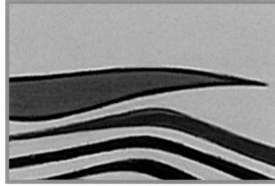

American bittern / alcaraván americano

cactus bee / abejorro

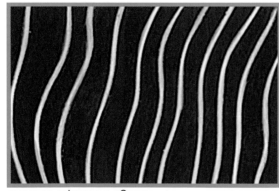

bongo / antílope africano

tiger / tigre

Florida tree snail / caracol de árbol de Florida

striped skunk / moteta rayada

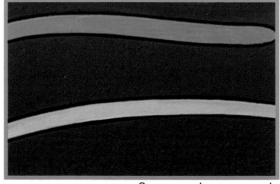

phantasmal poison frog / rana venenosa tricolor

mackerel tabby / gato atigrado

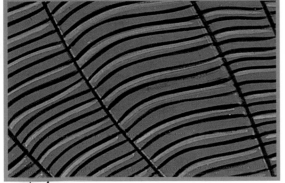

turkey / pavo

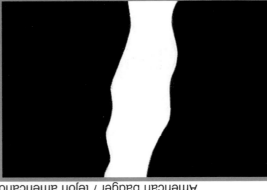

American badger / tejón americano

purple-striped jellyfish / medusa ortiga de mar

eastern garter snake / serpiente de jarretera

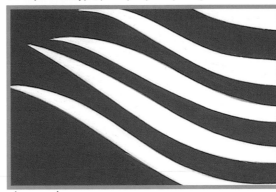

okapi / okapi

zebra swallowtail butterfly / mariposa cebra

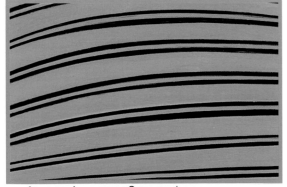

striped surgeonfish / pez cirujano

common zebra / cebra común

zebra moray eel / morena cebra

Malayan tapir / tapir malayo

Turn the book upside down
to read the correct answers.

Dale la vuelta al libro y encontrarás
las respuestas correctas.

Stinging tentacles on the adult **purple-striped jellyfish** can kill or paralyze prey. Its brightly colored stripes may alert predators to stay away. (California coast of the Pacific Ocean; invertebrate)

Una picadura de los tentáculos de la **medusa ortiga de mar** adulta puede paralizar y hasta matar a su presa. Puede que sus rayas chillonas adviertan a los predadores y los mantengan alejados. (California, costa del océano Pacífico; invertebrado)

The striped pattern on the **eastern garter snake** helps it go unseen while it slithers along the grassy ground. (North America; reptile)

El patrón rayado de la **serpiente de jarretera** le permite pasar inadvertida al arrastrarse por entre la hierba. (América del Norte; reptil)

The **ring-tailed lemur** uses its distinctive black-and-white striped tail to communicate, sometimes raising it like a flag to keep group members together. (Madagascar, off the coast of Africa; mammal)

El **lémur de cola anillada** usa su inconfundible rabo blanco y negro para comunicarse. A veces lo eleva como una bandera para mantener juntos a los miembros del grupo. (Madagascar, frente a la costa de África; mamífero)

Striped feathers on the **American bittern** help camouflage it among the dense reed beds in which it lives. Though its call is booming, the bird prefers to stay hidden. (North and Central America; bird)

Las plumas rayadas del **alcaraván americano** lo camuflan entre los densos juncos donde habita. Aunque tiene un llamado estridente, el alcaraván prefiere permanecer oculto. (América del Norte y Central; ave)

The **Florida tree snail** lives on smooth-barked hardwood trees and feeds on the fungi and algae that grow there. The reason for its swirling stripes is unknown. (Southeastern United States; mollusk)

El **caracol de árbol de Florida** habita árboles de madera dura y corteza lisa, y se alimenta de los hongos y las algas que crecen en ellos. La razón de sus rayas arremolinadas se desconoce. (Sureste de Estados Unidos; molusco)

Stripes on the **zebra moray eel** may help it blend with its surroundings and recognize other eels of its own kind. Its stripes increase in number as it grows larger. (Indo-Pacific Ocean and Red Sea; fish)

Las rayas de la **morena cebra** probablemente la ayudan a integrarse en su entorno y a reconocer a otras de su misma especie. A medida que crece, el número de rayas aumenta. (Océano Índico-Pacífico y Mar Rojo; pez)

The **tiger**, the largest wildcat in the world, has stripes that allow it to hide among tall grasses as it stalks its prey. (South and Southeast Asia, China, and the Russian Far East; mammal)

El **tigre** es el felino salvaje más grande del mundo. Sus rayas le permiten esconderse en la maleza mientras acecha a sus presas. (Sur y sureste de Asia, China y la zona más oriental de Rusia; mamífero)

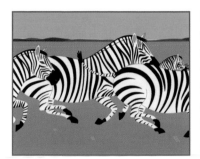

Black and white stripes on the **common zebra** make it hard for predators to distinguish a single animal from the herd. No two zebras' stripes are exactly alike. (Africa; mammal)

Las rayas en blanco y negro de la **cebra común** hacen que sus enemigos no logren distinguir a un animal entre los demás de la manada. No hay dos cebras con rayas exactamente iguales. (África; mamífero)

Two black stripes help conceal the eyes of the **American badger**, making it less visible to its enemies as it hunts for food in the tall prairie grass. (North America; mammal)

El **tejón americano** tiene dos rayas negras que ocultan sus ojos, haciéndolo menos visible a sus enemigos mientras caza sus alimentos entre las altas hierbas de la pradera. (América del Norte; mamífero)

Vertical white stripes on the **bongo** break up its body outline so that it blends with its wooded surroundings. (Africa; mammal)

Las rayas verticales del **antílope africano** dividen el contorno de su cuerpo de modo que se mezcla con el entorno arbolado. (África; mamífero)

The black and yellow stripes on the **cactus bee** may serve as a warning to predators. If threatened, the bee will defend itself by injecting venom from its stinger. (North and South America; arthropod)

Las rayas negras y amarillas del **abejorro** pueden servir de advertencia para los depredadores. Si es amenazado, se defiende inyectando veneno a través de su aguijón. (América del Norte y del Sur; artrópodo)

A baby **Malayan tapir** has stripes to help it hide in the forest. As the tapir grows up, the stripes fade away. (Southeast Asia; mammal)

El **tapir malayo** nace con rayas que disimulan su presencia en el bosque. A medida que crece, las rayas van desapareciendo. (Sureste de Asia; mamífero)

Bright stripes on the **phantasmal poison frog** are a signal to potential predators that it is toxic. Scientists have used the poison produced by this frog to help develop effective painkillers for humans. (South America; amphibian)

Las llamativas rayas de la **rana venenosa tricolor** son una señal de su toxicidad para los posibles depredadores. Usando el veneno producido por esta rana los científicos han desarrollado eficaces calmantes para los seres humanos. (América del Sur; anfibio)

Stripes on the wings of the **zebra swallowtail butterfly** create visual confusion for predators, so they don't know which part of the butterfly's body to attack. (North America; arthropod)

Las rayas en las alas de la **mariposa cebra** confunden visualmente a los depredadores de modo que no saben qué parte del cuerpo de la mariposa atacar. (América del Norte; artrópodo)

The **striped skunk** has bold stripes that warn other animals to stay away. When a skunk is threatened, it produces an oily, smelly spray that repels most predators. (North America; mammal)

La **mofeta rayada** tiene llamativas rayas que advierten a otros animales que no deben acercarse. Cuando se siente amenazada, la mofeta produce una sustancia grasienta y apestosa que repele a la mayoría de los depredadores. (América del Norte; mamífero)

Many fishes, such as the **striped surgeonfish**, **sixline wrasse**, and **oriental sweetlips**, have colorful stripes that identify them to other fishes of their own kind and may also help camouflage them among the coral reefs. (Indo-Pacific Ocean; fish)

Muchos peces, tales como el **pez cirujano**, el **labrido de seis líneas** y el **roncador oriental**, tienen rayas que los identifican a otros de su especie y también puede que ayuden a camuflarlos entre los arrecifes de coral. (Océano Índico-Pacífico; pez)

White, horizontal stripes on the legs of the **okapi** help it hide from predators in the dense jungle. This rare forest giraffe is a fast runner and a good jumper. (Africa; mammal)

Las rayas blancas horizontales del **okapi,** lo ayudan a esconderse de los depredadores en la jungla. Esta rara jirafa del bosque es muy ágil corriendo y saltando. (África; mamífero)

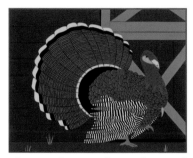

To attract a female, the male **turkey** displays his striped, fan-shaped tail feathers and produces a distinctive gobble that can be heard a mile away. (North America; bird)

Para atraer a las hembras, el **pavo** macho despliega las plumas de su cola en forma de abanico y emite un penetrante graznido que se puede oír hasta a una milla de distancia. (América del Norte; ave)

The **mackerel tabby** and some other domestic cats retain the striped pattern of the African wildcat, their direct ancestor. (worldwide; mammal)

El **gato atigrado**, y algunos otros gatos domésticos, conservan las rayas de los gatos salvajes africanos de los cuales descienden. (Mundo entero; mamífero)